17 COLLECTED EASY QUINTETS

THE CANADIAN BRASS

HAL•LEONARD®

WHEN JESUS WEPT

Trumpet in B-flat I

Arranged by Charles Sayre

William Billings
(1746-1800)

*Legato throughout

KITTERY

Trumpet in B-flat I

Arranged by Charles Sayre

William Billings
(1746-1800)

HOSANNA!

Trumpet in B-flat I

Arranged by Walter H. Barnes

Giovanni Pierluigi da Palestrina
(ca. 1525-1594)

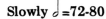

Slowly ♩=72-80

NON NOBIS DOMINE

Trumpet in B-flat I

Arranged by Walter H. Barnes

William Byrd
(ca. 1540-1623)

Smoothly ♩=84

AH, HOLY JESUS
(Herzliebster Jesu)

Trumpet in B-flat I

Arranged by Richard Walters

Johannes Crüger
(1598-1662)

ETERNAL FATHER, STRONG TO SAVE
(Melita)

Trumpet in B-flat I

Arranged by Richard Walters

John B. Dykes
(1823-1876)

VICTORIOUS LOVE
(Amor Vittorioso)

Trumpet in B-flat I

Arranged by Charles Sayre

Giovanni Giacomo Gastoldi
(ca. 1554-1609)

Play through the piece twice.

IN THE HALL OF THE MOUNTAIN KING

from *Peer Gynt*

Trumpet in B-flat I

Arranged by Charles Sayre

Edvard Grieg
(1843-1907)

MENUET
from *Music for the Royal Fireworks*

Trumpet in B-flat I

Arranged by Walter H. Barnes

George Frideric Handel
(1685-1759)

O SACRED HEAD
(O Haupt voll Blut und Wunden)

Trumpet in B-flat I

Harmonization by Johann Sebastian Bach
Arranged by Charles Sayre

Hans Leo Hassler
(1564-1612)

*Legato tongue throughout unless otherwise slurred.

BREAK FORTH, O BEAUTEOUS HEAVENLY LIGHT
(Ermuntre Dich)

Trumpet in B-flat I

Harmonization by Johann Sebastian Bach
Arranged by Charles Sayre

Johann Schop
(ca. 1600-1667)

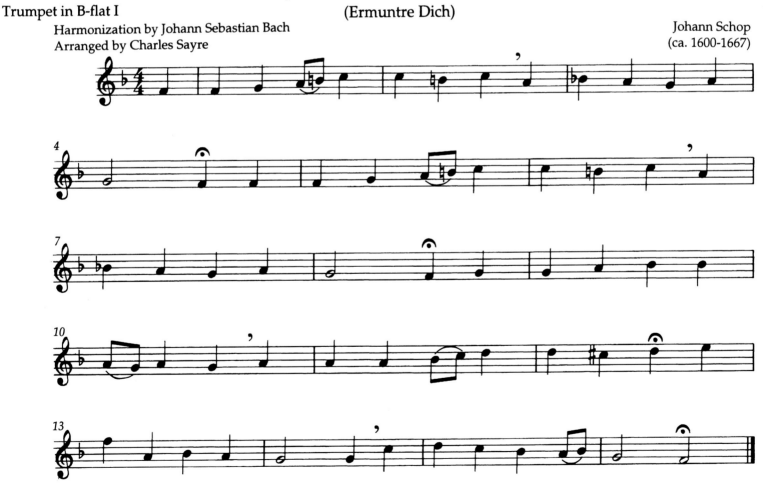

AUSTRIAN HYMN

from String Quartet No. 62 "Emperor" in C Major, Op. 76, No. 3

Trumpet in B-flat I

Arranged by Charles Sayre

Franz Joseph Haydn
(1732-1809)

A MIGHTY FORTRESS
(Ein feste Burg ist unser Gott)

Trumpet in B-flat I

Arranged by Richard Walters

Martin Luther
(1483-1546)

CANON

Trumpet in B-flat I

Arranged by Charles Sayre

Thomas Tallis
(ca. 1505-1585)

BEAUTIFUL SAVIOR
(Schönster Herr Jesu)
from *Münster Gesangbuch, 1677*

Trumpet in B-flat I

Arranged by Richard Walters

Traditional

CHRIST THE LORD IS RISEN TODAY

from *Lyra Davidica*, 1708

Trumpet in B-flat I

Arranged by Richard Walters

Traditional

WE GATHER TOGETHER
(Kremser)

Trumpet in B-flat I

Arranged by Richard Walters

Traditional

THE CANADIAN BRASS

CONTENTS

SCORE AND PARTS AVAILABLE SEPARATELY:
Conductor's Score   50486953
Trumpet 2 in B-flat   50486949
Horn in F   50486950
Trombone   50486951
Tuba   50486952

ALSO AVAILABLE IN THIS SERIES:
14 Collected Intermediate Quintets   50486959

HAL•LEONARD® CORPORATION
7777 W. BLUEMOUND RD. P.O. BOX 13819 MILWAUKEE, WI 53213

U.S. $9.99
ISBN 978-1-4234-8309-0

HL50486948

www.canbrass.com
www.halleonard.com

8-84088-39295-6

50999